303

TRICKY

CHECKMATES

ABOUT THE AUTHORS

FRED WILSON
Fred Wilson is among the finest chess teachers and authors. He has authored *303 Tricky Chess Tactics* with Bruce Alberston for Cardoza Publishing, as well as three other books: *A Picture History of Chess, 101 Questions on How to Play Chess,* and *202 Surprising Mates* (with Alberston). He has also edited *Classical Chess Matches:1907-1913,* and *Lesser-Known Chess Masterpieces: 1906-1915.* He is also the owner of Fred Wilson Chess Books in New York City.

BRUCE ALBERSTON
Bruce Alberston is a well-known chess trainer and teacher in the New York city area and has recently written and narrated the best-selling CD-ROM, *Quick Kills on the Chessboard,* and collaborated with Fred Wilson on *202 Surprising Mates* and *303 Tricky Chess Tactics* with Wilson. Alberston did significant research and analysis for Bruce Pandolfini (who has written 17 books for Simon & Shuster).

303

TRICKY

CHECKMATES

Fred Wilson & Bruce Alberston

CARDOZA PUBLISHING

ACKNOWLEDGMENTS

Special thanks to our secret resource, Michele Lance. Michele stopped short of chopping wood to make paper, but she was involved in everything else. Others who contributed positions, checked solutions, or made useful suggestions include: Christopher Mayfield, David MacEnulty, Adam Marcus, Gregory Caesar, Dan Satterwaite, Ben Schanback, Jeff Tannenbaum, Tom Schrade, Mike Senkiewicz, Emmitt Jefferson, Andy Ansel, Andrew Fox, Glen Hart, Ned Wall, Oshon Temple, Rita Kelly, Marianna Loosemore and Larry Grasso.

SECOND EDITION

Library of Congress Catalog Card No: 2002101329
ISBN: 1-58042-040-0

Visit our new web site (www.cardozapub.com) or write us for a full list of Cardoza books, advanced, and computer strategies.

CARDOZA PUBLISHING
PO Box 1500, Cooper Station, New York, NY 10276
Phone (718)743-5229 • Fax (718)743-8284
email: cardozapub@aol.com
www.cardozapub.com

TABLE OF CONTENTS

INTRODUCTION

*A thorough understanding of the typical mating continuations makes the most sacrificial combinations leading up to them not only not difficult, but almost a matter of course. – **Tarrasch***

*It is a mistake to think that combination is solely a question of talent, and that it cannot be acquired. – **Reti***

"I can't believe I missed a mate in two!" How many, many times have you said this to yourself during your chessplaying career? Too often, I bet. Deep down you know that missed tactical threats or opportunities are the biggest hindrance to your improvement at chess.

Recently, one of us, Fred Wilson, reached the following position as White:

White, although a Pawn ahead, has a difficult position because of Black's heavy artillery on the g and h files, pointing at his King. Among Black's threats, were it his move, are 1... Qxh3 with a winning attack. White's g Pawn is pinned against his King by the Black Rook on g8.

White had a choice between 1. Qf3, which, although it defends against possible sacrifices on g2, does lose the h Pawn to 1... Qxh3! 2. Qxh3 Rxh3, and the seemingly safe, 1. Kh1, which is what he did.

What would you do now if you were Black?

Answer: **1... Qxh3+! gxh3 2. Rxh3#.** That's right! An experienced player fell into a classic *corridor mate*, wherein the doomed King is mated by a major piece (Queen or Rook) on a rank or file, because there are no legal escape squares on the adjacent ranks or files, and no possible interpositions.

The possibility of this classic mating pattern, (like the notorious *back rank mate* except here mate occurs on the h file rather then the 1st or 8th rank,) should have been recognized by White, even if it was brought about by a Queen sacrifice!

So, what's the answer? How can we learn to stop overlooking mating combinations available to us, and threatened against us? There is only one way: to study different types of checkmating combinations over and over again until we are thoroughly familiar with the tactics and typical groups of pieces involved in successfully implementing them.

While in the past, it was believed that the ability to create attractive checkmating combinations must be a born gift, nowadays modern teaching experience has established that consistent training through solving standard checkmating positions, no matter how difficult, will improve any player's "feel" for discovering correct, and even brilliant, checkmating attacks.

What we have done in *303 Tricky Checkmates* is to assemble a collection of *forced* checkmates in 2, 3 and 4 moves, which we believe you will find both instructive and entertaining. We have purposely used very large, clear diagrams so you will not be discouraged from really trying to visualize possible variations.

We have also intentionally included 100 positions (mates 101-150 and 251-300), in which Black is to play and force checkmate in two or three moves. We believe it is essential that you become comfortable with looking at positions from Black's perspective and solving tough tactical problems from that side.

Our classifcation system is quite direct in that we most often tell you, under the "theme column" in the introductions to Chapters One and Three, exactly what pieces and/

or Pawns are creating the mate. For instance, Position No. 17 in Chapter One is a classic Rook plus Bishop corridor mate on the 8th rank and we urge you to look at it right now and solve it!

Hint: the solution begins with a **quiet move,** a move that is neither a check nor a capture, which is why quiet moves are often the hardest to find.

Queen support mate simply means that you are mating the enemy King by placing your Queen next to it, with another one of your pieces or Pawns also attacking the mating square which you have just placed your Queen on. An example of this is the following position where, with White to move, the Spanish master Vilardebo missed an opportunity to checkmate one of the world's greatest players, Richard Reti, at the First Chess Olympiad, London 1927.

What would you have played? Notice that Black's Queen is what we call **overloaded** in that it has to defend against mates on both h8 and f7. We hope you found the answer: **1. Rh8+!** (a classic *deflection*, making the Queen give up her defense of f7). **1...Qxh8 forced, 2. Qxf7#.**

A **discovery** is any move by a piece or Pawn which opens a line of fire onto the enemy King, via a rank, file or diagonal, from a piece lurking behind the just moved unit. The most devastating discoveries are usually **double checks**, as in the example below where White mates in three moves.

This looks really tough, but during an offhand game in Paris, 1878, Maczulsky created a spectacular checkmate against Kolisch by means of a deadly discovered double check: **1. Qd8+!! Kxd8; 2. Bg5+ Ke8; 3. Rd8#.**

Although you may already know what a *pin* is in chess, you may not be sure how pins can be used tactically to force checkmate. We suggest you go immediately to Positions 79 and 80 in Chapter One. In each of these examples, White forces mate in two moves by creating a murderous pin by sacrificing a piece.

Now, we come to what is probably the most difficult tactical concept of all, especially when it is used to force checkmate, namely the "dreaded" zugswang. **Zugswang** basically means "compulsion to move". The losing side must make a move, but would rather not because the only legal moves available cause immediate loss. Consider the following:

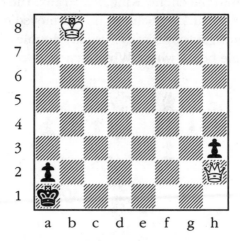

It is White's move. Would you grab the h Pawn or...? We certainly hope not because then the position is theoretically a draw! But, perhaps you noticed that after 1. Qc2!, Black is not only not *stalemated* as he would have been had there been no h Pawn, but is, in fact, in *zugswang*, as his only legal move 1... h2, allows 2. Qc1#.

Finally, you will notice that throughout the book there are an abundance of sacrifices. Particularly evident and exciting are the Queen sacrifices to open lines of attack, to annihilate defenders, to draw off or deflect defenders, or to attract the King to the mating square.

The whole tactical canon of chess is condensed in the challenging mates you will find in this book.

Enjoy.

Fred Wilson & Bruce Alberston

CHAPTER 1

WHITE TO MOVE AND MATE IN TWO

WHITE MATES IN TWO

"White mates in two" indicates that White moves first, Black responds, and White delivers checkmate on his second move. Computer people think of this as three individual moves, or three-ply. Chess folks, accustomed to thinking in move pairs, refer to this as a two-mover. Technically, it's just a move and a half, as Black never gets to make his second move.

ORGANIZATION

The layout of Chapter One is by theme. Typical mating configurations and strategems are grouped together to aid familiarization. Here's what to look for:

Problems	Theme
1-13	Back rank and other corridor mates
14-27	Rook and Bishop corridors
28-39	Diagonal mates with Queen and Bishop or Rook and Bishop or only a Bishop!
40-48	Bishop and Knight Mates
49-64	Support mates with the Queen
65-73	Knight checkmates
74-78	Pawn mates and promotion
79-92	Pins and discoveries
93-100	Quiet moves and Zugswang

SOLVING HINTS

Since the goal is checkmate and you have only two moves to work with, you'll need to operate with forcing moves. The most forcing moves are also the most violent moves: checks, captures and immediate threats of mate. Also, don't be afraid to sacrifice. Material becomes irrelevant when you're hunting down the enemy King.

Go to it now and get the enemy King.

1.

2.

3.

4.

5.

6.

7.

8.

9.

10.

11.

12.

13.

14.

15.

16.

17.

18.

19.

20.

21.

22.

23.

24.

25.

26.

27.

28.

29.

30.

31.

32.

33.

34.

35.

36.

37.

38.

39.

40.

41.

42.

43.

44.

45.

46.

47.

48.

49.

50.

51.

52.

53.

54.

55.

56.

57.

58.

59.

60.

61.

62.

63.

64.

65.

66.

67.

68.

69.

70.

71.

72.

73.

74.

75.

76.

77.

78.

79.

80.

81.

82.

83.

84.

85.

86.

87.

88.

89.

90.

91.

92.

93.

94.

95.

96.

97.

98.

99.

100.

CHAPTER 2

BLACK TO MOVE AND MATE IN TWO

BLACK MATES IN TWO

Here Black gets to make the first move, or the *key move* as it is sometimes called. White replies, and Black administers checkmate on his second move. There's nothing unusual about viewing the position from Black's perspective. In chess games, you'll have the Black pieces half the time. And Black also wins his share of the games.

ORGANIZATION

The mates are organized randomly, deliberately so. You're expected to see your way without any prompting. But here at least, as opposed to an actual game situation, you have the advantage of knowing mate is imminent.

In general, the problems in this section are harder than those in the previous one. More imagination is required and there are more side variations to consider. By this stage, however, most of the patterns should already be familiar, so it's a matter of applying what you already know.

SOLVING HINTS

As in the last chapter, forcing moves are the order of the day. Checks and captures with checks abound. Material sacrifice is by now a commonplace occurrence. The idea is to make the position bend to your will. Forcing moves will do it.

Problem #132 comes from our dirty tricks department. You'll need to know two things: the *en passant* capture, and White's last move, b2-b4.

Positions #130 and #140 are composed problems. They are included here more for their curiosity than for anything else. In each, Black places a piece on a square where it can be captured in multiple ways. Each mode of capture weakens the White defense in some fashion, allowing Black to mate. A methodical approach to these mates work best.

You are ready to begin Chapter Two. The objective is the White monarch. Go after him.

101.

102.

103.

104.

105.

106.

107.

108.

109.

110.

111.

112.

113.

114.

115.

116.

117.

118.

119.

120.

121.

122.

123.

124.

125.

126.

127.

128.

129.

130.

131.

132.

133.

134.

135.

136.

137.

138.

139.

140.

141.

142.

143.

144.

145.

146.

147.

148.

149.

150.

CHAPTER 3

WHITE TO MOVE AND MATE IN THREE

WHITE MATES IN THREE

In this chapter, it is White's turn to initiate the action: White moves, Black moves, White moves, Black moves, White's third move is checkmate. White uses moves one and two to open lines for his pieces, eliminate defenders, take away escape squares from the enemy King – in short, everything necessary to insure that move three is mate.

ORGANIZATION

The fundamental ideas of chess are fairly constant, thus, the catagories in this chapter look pretty much like those in Chapter One. But the numerous ways of implementing those basic ideas is where these mates get interesting.

SOLVING HINTS

We've advanced from the two mover to the three mover. In many instances, this is merely a lengthening of the mating process, a one move extension of a two move idea. Number 160 is a case in point. At its core, #160 is essentially the same as the two-mover, #15. But just as often, there is an extra dimension, a concept that cannot be carried out in less than three moves.

Your task then: extend and conceptualize to mate.

151.

152.

153.

154.

155.

156.

157.

158.

159.

160.

161.

162.

163.

164.

165.

166.

167.

168.

169.

170.

171.

172.

173.

174.

175.

176.

177.

178.

179.

180.

181.

182.

183.

184.

185.

186.

187.

188.

189.

190.

191.

192.

193.

194.

195.

196.

197.

198.

199.

200.

201.

202.

203.

204.

205.

206.

207.

208.

209.

210.

211.

212.

213.

214.

215.

216.

217.

218.

219.

220.

221.

222.

223.

224.

225.

226.

227.

228.

229.

230.

231.

232.

233.

234.

235.

236.

237.

238.

239.

240.

241.

242.

243.

244.

245.

246.

247.

248.

249.

250.

CHAPTER 4

BLACK TO MOVE AND MATE IN THREE

BLACK MATES IN THREE
It's Black's turn again. The sequence is Black, White, Black, White, Black. This third Black move is mate.

The problems in this section are harder than those in the preceding chapter. Black's job always seems to be tougher than White's due to White's inherent advantage in going first. More ingenuity is required, more calculation as well. But you should be up to the task.

ORGANIZATION
The positions have been randomized for the greatest challenges.

SOLVING HINTS
The time has come to give away the biggest secret of all: the answers are in the back of the book. So, if you get stuck on a mate, look it up. Then let some time go by, come back, and try again.

251.

252.

253.

254.

255.

256.

257.

258.

259.

260.

261.

262.

263.

264.

265.

266.

267.

268.

269.

270.

271.

272.

273.

274.

275.

276.

277.

278.

279.

280.

281.

282.

283.

284.

285.

286.

287.

288.

289.

290.

291.

292.

293.

294.

295.

296.

297.

298.

299.

300.

CHAPTER 5

WHITE TO MOVE AND MATE IN FOUR

WHITE MATES IN FOUR

You are about to enter the exalted realm of the four mover. White goes first, Black responds, you know the rest. Mate comes with White's fourth move.

Battle-hardened by your journey through the tricky mates in this book, you are no doubt expecting a reward for all your noble efforts. The big payoff will come when you apply what you've learned to your own games. It's either that or wait for our next book. Meanwhile, we offer a few tasty morsels for your last challenges.

301.

302.

303.

SOLUTIONS

#1. **1. Ng6+ fxg6 2. Qe8#**

#2. **1. Qf6** *and* **2. Rg8#**

#3. **1. Qxe5+**
   (A) 1...Kg8 2. Qg7#
   (B) 1...Rxe5 2. Rxd8#

#4. **1. R1e8** (*threatens* **2. Rxg8#**)
   1...Rxe8 2. Rxe8#

#5. **1. Rh8+ Kxh8 2. Rf8#**

#6. **1. Qb8+ Kxb8 2. Rd8#**

#7. **1. Nf6** (*threatens* **2. Qh7#**)
   1...Bxf6 2. Qxh6#

#8. **1. Rxf6+**
   (A) 1...gxf6 2. Qxf6#
   (B) 1...Ke7 2. Rf7#
   Double check and mate.

#9. **1. Qxh5+ Kxh5 2. Rh7#**

#10. **1. Qxh6+ (A) 1...Kg8 2. Rg5#**
   (B) 1...Kxh6 2. Rh5#

#11. **1. Rh1+ Kg3 2. Rh3#**

#12. **1. Ne5+ Kxd4 2. Rd2#**

#13. **1. Rhh7** *and* **2. Rhe7#**

#14. **1. Qxe8 Kxe8 2. Rd8#**

#15. **1. Bg6+ Kg8 2. Re8#**

#16. **1. Bh6** *and* **2. Rxf8#**

#17. **1. Rf1** *and* **2. Rf8#**

#18. **1. Qxe6+**
   (A) 1...Kh8 2. Qxe8#
   (B) 1...Rxe6 2. Rf8#

#19. **1. Rxh6+**
   (A) 1...Kxh6 2. Qh4#
   (B) 1...Kg8 2. Rh8#

#20. **1. Qxh6+**
   (A) 1...Kg8 2. Qh8#
   (B) 1...Kxh6 2. Rh2#

#21. **1. Qxh7+ Kxh7 2. Bf8#**

#22. **1. Bh6+ Kh7 2. Bf8#**

#23. **1. Qxh5+ gxh5 2. Rh6#**

#24. **1. Qxh7+ Rxh7 2.Rxh7#**

#25. **1. Rh8+ Bxh8 2. Rh7#**

#26. **1. Re1+ Kd6 2. Re6#**

#27. **1. Qxf5+ Kxf5 2. Rf4#**

#28. **1. g3+ Kxg3 2. Qf2#**

#29. **1. Bb2+ Kxe4 2. Qf3#**

#30. **1. Rc8+ Qxc8 2. Qxd6#**

#31. **1. Qxe6+**
  (A) 1...Qe7 2. Qxe7#
  (B) 1...fxe6 2. Bg6#

#32. **1. Qxf6+**
  (A) 1...Qf7 2. Qxf7#
  (B) 1...gxf6 2. Bh6#

#33. **1. Qxf6+ gxf6 2. Bxf6#**

#34. **1. Bxf7+ Ke7 2. Bg5#**

#35. **1. Rf8+ Bxf8 2. Bg6#**

#36. **1. Qxh7+ Nxh7 2. Bxh7#**

#37. **1. Qxg6+ hxg6 2. Bxg6#**

#38. **1. Qxh5+ Rxh5 2. Bg6#**

#39. **1. Kh2** (*threatens* **2. g3#**)
  1...g4 2. Be7#

#40. **1. Bc2+ Kh6 2. Nf7#**

#41. **1. Ngf7+ Kg7 2. Bh6#**

#42. **1. Qh8+ Rxh8 2. Nf6#**

#43. **1. Rd7+ Bxd7 2. Nf7#**
#44. **1. Rxb7+ Nxb7 2. Na6#**

#45. **1. Qe8+ Qxe8 2. Nxf6#**

#46. **1. Nxd6+ Nxd6 2. Ne7#**

#47. **1. Qf8+ Rxf8 2. Ne7#**

#48. **1. Qxh6** (*threatens* **2. Qxg7#**).
  1...gxh6 2. Nxh6#

#49. **1. Qh6+ gxh6 2. Rh7#**

#50. **1. Qxh7+ Kxh7 2. Rh4#**

#51. **1. Nf5+ Kf8 2. Ra8#**
  Anastasia's Mate

#52. **1. Qf8+**
  (A) 1...Rxf8 2. Ne7#
  (B) 1...Kxf8 2. Rh8#

#53. **1. Qf7+ Bxf7 2. Nd7#**

#54. **1. Qe7+ Rxe7 2. Nf6#**

#55. **1. Qxh7+ Nxh7 2. Ng6#**

#56. **1. Qe2+ Kg5 2. Qg4#**

#57. **1. Rxa6+ bxa6 2. Qa7#**

#58. **1. a4+ Kxa4 2. Qb3#**

#59. **1. Rf8+ Qxf8 2. Qxh7#**

#60. **1. Qh8+ Kf7 2. Qxg7#**

#61. **1. Bxh7+ Qxh7 2. Qf8#**

#62. **1. Rxa7+ Kxa7 2. Qxb6#**

#63. **1. Bf6** *and* **2. Qe7#**

#64. **1. Rxg7+ Kxg7 2. Qh7#**

#65. **1. Nxe5 Rxe5 2. Nf4#**

#66. **1. Qg8+ Rxg8 2. Nf7#**
The old Smothered Mate

#67. **1. Qxh7+ Bxh7 2. Nf7#**

#68. **1. Qxb8+ Qxb8 2. Nb6#**

#69. **1. Qxc7+ Rxc7 2. Nb6#**

#70. **1. Rf5+ (A) 1...Rg5 2. Rxg5#**
(B) 1...N(B)xf5 2. Nf4#

#71. **1. Qg7+ Rxg7 2. Nh6#**

#72. **1. Qe4+ Kxe4 2. Nf6#**

#73. **1. Rg8+ Rxg8 2. Nf7#**

#74. **1. e8/N+ Ke6 2. d5#**

#75. **1. fxg7+ Kg8 2. gxh8/Q#**
*Also a pin mate, as the f7 -
Knight cannot capture.*

#76. **1. Qg7+ Kxg7 2. h8/Q#**

#77. **1. Rh7+ Kg5 2. h4#**

#78. **1. Qxh5+ Bxh5 2. g5#**

#79. **1. Ra4 Qxa4 2. Qh3#**

#80. **1. Bc5** *(threatens 2. B(Q)xe7#)*
1...Qxc5 2. Qe8#

#81. **1. Qxf7+ Kh7 2. Qh5#**

#82. **1. Qxh6+ Kg8 2. Q(R)xg7#**

#83. **1. Qxf7+**
(A) 1...Kh8 2. Qxf8#
(B) 1...Rxf7 2. Rc8#

#84. **1. Rxh7+ (A) 1...Bxh7 2. Nf7#**
(B) 1....Kxh7 2. Rh3#

#85. **1. Qg6** *(threatens 2. Qxh6#)*
1...Rf8 2. Qxg7#

#86. **1. Rh6+ e6 2. Nf5#**

#87. **1. Qg6+ Qxg6 2. Rh4#**

#88. **1. Be7+ Kh8 2. Bf6#**

#89. **1. Rf8+ Kxf8 2. Qf7#**

#90. **1. Qh7+ Kxh7 2. Bf7#**

#91. **1. Qg7+ Kxg7 2. Rxg6#**

#92. **1. Qxd8+ Kxd8 2. Rg8#**

#93. **1. c4 Ka5 2. Qa7#**
*The en passent capture, 1...bxc3, is
illegal, as the b4 pawn is pinned.*

#94. **1. f4** *and* **2. Nd2#**

#95. **1. Kh6** *and* **2. Rd8#**
*Not 1. Kf6? cxb5! and the d6-Rook
is pinned.*

#96. **1. Kc4** *(threatens 2. Ra1#)*
1...Bxe5 2. Ra6#

#97. **1. Kc2** *and* **2. Re1#**

#98. **1. Nf5** (*threatens* **2. Qg7#**)
    1...gxf5 2.Qf6#

#99. **1. Ba7 c6 2. Bb8#**
    The Switchback theme.

#100. **1. Rh7** *and* **2. R(x)d7#**
    Black is in zugswang and his
    rook has to give up control of d7.

#101. **1...Bh3+ (A) 2. Kxh3 Qg4#**
    (B) 2. Kg1 Qd4#

#102. **1...Qh6+ (A) 2. Kxh6 Bd2#**
    (B) 2. Bxh6 Bd8#
    (C) 2 Kh4 Be1#

#103. **1...Ba3** *and* **2...Rc1#**

#104. **1...Bxf5** (*threatening* **2...Rh3#**)
    2. Rxf5 R7g4#

#105. **1...Qxe2**
    (A) 2. Rexe2 Rf1#
    (B) 2. Rhxe2 Nf2#
    (C) 2. Qxe2 Nb2#

#106. **1...Bd5+** *and* **2...Qe3#**

#107. **1...Nc3 (A) 2. Bxb8 Rxa2#**
    (B) 2. Qxa7 Rb1#

#108. **1...Qg1+ 2. Nxg1 Nf2#**

#109. **1...Kh7** *and* **2...g6#**

#110. **1...Qg1+**
    (A) 2. Kf3 Bb7#
    (B) 2. Kd2 Ne4#

#111. **1...Bxb3+**
    (A) 2. Kxb3 Qa4#
    (B) 2. Kb1 Qa2#
    (C) 2. Kd2 Qh6#

#112. **1...Bc3+**
    (A) 2. Kxc3 d1/N#
    (B) 2. Kb1 d1/Q#

#113. **1...Ng3+ 2. hxg3 Rh5#**

#114. **1...Rb2** *and* **2...Rc6#**

#115. **1...Bf4+ (A) 2. Qxf4 Qa5#**
    (B) 2. Re3 Rd1#

#116. **1...Qa6 (A) 2. g6 Qxg6#**
    (B) 2. e6 Qxe6#
    (C) 2. Ke4 Qd3#

#117. **1...Qf1+ (A) 2. Kxf1 Rh1#**
    (B) 2. Rxf1 Ne2#

#118. **1...Nb3+ (A) 2. Bxb3 Qa1#**
    (B) 2. Kb1 Ned2#

#119. **1...b3 (A) 2. cxb3 Kxb3#**
    (B) 2. Ba2 Kxc2#

#120. **1...Qa4+ 2. Kd3 Nc1#**

#121. **1...b5+** *and* **2...Qa6#**

#122. **1...Rxe2** *and* **2...Be8#**

#123. **1...Rf5+ (A) 2. Kxe4 Re5#**
    (B) 2. Kc4 Nd2#

#124. **1...Qa7** *and* **2...Rxf1#**

#125. 1...gxh1/B 2. Kxg1 Ke2#

#126. 1...Bb2 (A) 2. Bxb4 Qa1#
(B) 2. Bxb2 Qa2#

#127. 1...Qg1+ 2. Kxg1 Re1#

#128. 1...Rxa3+ (A) 2. Kxa3 Qa1#
(B) 2. Qxa3 Qa5#
(C) 2. Kb5 a6#

#129. 1...Kh1 *zugswang.*
(A) 2. Ne2-*moves* Ng3#
(B) 2. Nc4-*moves* Ne3#

#130. 1...Qc4+
There are eight ways to take the Queen:
(A) 2. Kxc4 Re4#
(B) 2. Qxc4 Ne2#
(C) 2. R6xc4 Ne6#
(D) 2. R3xc4 Rxd3#
(E) 2. Bxc4 Nxc6#
(F) 2. Naxc4 Nxb5#
(G) 2. Nbxc4 Rd5#
(H) 2. dxc4 Re4#

#131. 1...Nf3 (*threatens* 2...Nh2#)
2. gxf3 Qh3#

#132. *White has just played* 1. b2-b4
allowing the en passant capture:
1...cxb3+ 2. Ka1 Bb2#

#133. 1...Rxh3+ (A) 2. Kxh3 Qh5#
(B) 2. gxh3 Qf2# *An epaulet mate.*

#134. 1...Nb3 *and* 2...Qa1#

#135. 1...Ng2 (*threatens* 2...Ne3#)
2. Kxg2 f1/Q#

#136. 1...Nd4+ (A) 2. Kf1 Qg2#
(B) 2. Bxd4 (*or* 2. Kd2)
2...Qd3#

#137. 1...Qxc5+ 2. Kxc5 Ne6#

#138. 1...Rxe4 (*threatens* 2...Re1# *and* 2...Ref4#)
(A) 2. Rxe4 Bxe4#
(B) 2. Rh8+ Re8#

#139. 1. Be3 *zugswang.*
(A) 2. Nb2 Bc5#
(B) 2. Nb4 Bc1#

#140. 1...Nd5 (*threatening* 2...Rd1#)
The Knight has to be taken and there are eight ways to do it:
(A) 2. Kxd5 Rd1#
(B) 2. Qxd5 Qa1#
(C) 2. Rxd5 Qxc4#
(D) 2. Bxd5 e5#
(E) 2. Ncxd5 Nxe6#
(F) 2. Nfxd5 Rxe4#
(G) 2. exd5 Be5#
(H) 2. cxd5 Qd3#

#141. 1.Qc4 (*threatens* 2...Qe2#)
(A) 2. Bd3 Qxc1#
(B) 2. Bd1 Qh4#

#142. 1...Rxf1+ 2. Kxf1 Qh1#

#143. 1...Rb4 *and* 2...Raxa4#

#144. 1...Rf5+
(A) 2. Kxf5 Qf6#
(B) 2. Ke3 Qe1#
A swallow's tail and an epaulet.

#145. 1...Qh3+
(A) 2. Kxh3 Bf1#
(B) 2. Kg1 Qf1#

#146. **1...Re2+ 2. Kxe2 Qd2#**
The Swallow's Tail mate, a close relative of the epaulet.

#147. **1...Qg2+ (A) 2. Qxg2 Ne2#**
(B) 2. Rxg2 Nh3#

#148. **1...Qe5** (*threatening* **2...Rd1#.**)
(A) 2. Qxh4+ Rxh4#
(B) 2. Qh2 Rf4#
(C) 2. Qe1 Rd2#
(D) 2. Kb2 Rc4#
(E) 2. exd4 Qxd4#

#149. **1...Rd1+ (A) 2. Nxd1 Qc4#**
(B) 2. Qe1 Rxe1#
(C) 2. Ke2 Nd4#

#150. **1...b5** (*threatens* **2...Rf1#**)
(A) 2. Qxb5 Qxb5#
(B) 2. c3 Qe4#

#151. **1.Nf4+ Kg8 2. Rag2+ Kf8**
3. Rh8#

#152. **1. Qg7+ Rxg7 2. Re8+ Rg8**
3. Rxg8#

#153. **1. Nh6+ gxh6 2. Rg3+ Kf7**
(or 2...Kh8 3. Rxf8#) 3. Re7#

#154. **1. Qxf6+ Rxf6**
(or 1...Kg8 2. Qg7#) 2. Rxd8+
Rf8 3. Rxf8#

#155. **1. Qxf7+ Rxf7 2. Rd8+ Rf8**
3.Rxf8#

#156. **1. Qd8 Rxd8 2. f8/Q+ Rxf8**
3. Rxf8#

#157. **1. Nh6+ gxh6 2. Rg4+ Kh8**
3. Rxf8#

#158. **1. Qxb8 Rxb8 2. e8/Q+ Rxe8**
3. Rxe8#

#159. **1. Qxd8+ Rxd8 2. Re8+ Rxe8**
3.Rxe8#

#160. **1. g6+ hxg6 2. fxg6+ Ke8**
3. Re8#

#161. **1. Nh5+ gxh5 2. Qg5+ Kf8**
3. Rd8#

#162. **1. Qh7+ Ka1 2. Qh8 Kb1**
3. Qh1#

#163. **1. Nd7+ Ka8 2. Rc5** (*threatens*
3. Ra5#) **2...Re5 3. Rc8#**

#164. **1. Qxh7+ Kxh7 2. Rh4+ Bxh4**
3.Rxh4#

#165. **1. Ng6+ hxg6 2. Qg1** *and*
3. Qh2#

#166. **1. Rxh6+ Kxh6 2. Qf4+** *and*
3. Qh2#

#167. **1. Bg8** (*threatens* **2. Rh7#**)
1...Rxg8 2. Rxg8+ Kh7 3.
R1g7#

#168. **1. Rg7+ Kh8 2. Rh7+ Kg8**
3. Rag7#

#169. **1. Qxh7+ Kxh7 2. Rh3+ Kg6**
3. Rg2#

#170. **1. Qh8+ Ke7 2. Ng6+ fxg6**
3. Qxg7#

#171. **1. Qg4+ Bg5 2. Qxg5+ fxg5
3. Rh8#**

#172. **1. Qh8+ Kxh8 2. Rxh5+ Kg8
3. Rh8#**

#173. **1. Qxb6+ cxb6 2. Rxb6+ Kc7
3. Rb7#**
The swallow's tail mate.

#174. **1. Qxf8+ Kxf8 2. Bh6+ Kg8
3. Re8#**

#175. **1. Qg7+ Bxg7 2. Rxd8+ Bf8
3. Rxf8#**

#176. **1. Rf4+ Kh8 2. Ng6+ hxg6
3.Rh4#**
*Greco's h-file corridor mate with
Bishop and heavy piece. It goes
back to 1619.*

#177. **1. Bf5** *followed by* **2. h4+** *and*
3. Rh7#

#178. **1. Bh6+ Kg8 2. Bxf7+ Kxf7
3. Qa2#**

#179. **1. Qc5+ Kd8 2. e7+ Kd7
3. Bf5#**

#180. **1. Qg7+ Ke8 2. Nd6+ cxd6
3. Bg6#**

#181. **1. Rxh6+ gxh6 2. Bb2+ Rf6
3. Bxf6#**

#182. **1. Bd8** *followed by*
2. b6+ cxb6
3. Bxb6# *Black can't stop it.*

#183. **1. Nf8+ Kh8 2. Qh7+ Nxh7
3. Ng6#**

#184. *The quiet move,* **1. Kf1,** *sets
things up:*
1...Kxh2 2. Bd6+ Kh1 3.Nf2#
*If Black plays a different first
move, White reverses with*
2. Nf2+ *and* **3. Bd6#**

#185. **1. Re8+ Kxe8 2. Rg8+ Ke7
3. Nf5#**

#186. **1. Ne8** (*threatens* **2. Rg7#**) **1...hxg4
2. Rg7+ (A) 2. ...Kf5 3. Nd6#
(B) 2. ...Kh5 3. Nxf6#**

#187. **1. Qxf7+ Rxf7 2. Rxf7+ Kh8
3. Ng6#**

#188. **1. Qxh6+ gxh6 (1...Kxh6 2. Rh1#)
2. Nf6+ Kh8 3. Rxg8#**
*The Arabian Rook and Knight
mate.*

#189. **1. Nc5+ Kb8 (1...Kd8 2. Qd7#)
2. Qc8+ (A) 2...Ka7 2. Qxb7#
(B) 2...Kxc8 3.Rf8#**

#190. **1. Ne7+ Kh8 2. Qxh7+ Kxh7
3. Rh4#** *Anastasia's mate.*

#191. **1. Qxg7+ Nxg7 2. Rh6+ Kg8
3. Ne7#**

#192. **1. Ne7+ Kh8 2. Qxh7+ Kxh7
3. Rh4#**

#193. **1. Qxf7+ Rxf7 2. Ng6+ Kg8
3. Rh8#**

#194. **1. Rh8+ Kxh8 2. Qh5+ Kg8
3. Qh7#**

#195. **1. Ra8+ Kxa8 2. Qa1+ Kb8
3. Qa7#**

#196. **1. Rh7+ Kxh7 2. Qf7+ Kh8
3. Qg7#**

#197. **1. Rxg5** (*threatens* **2. Qxg7#**)
1. ...hxg5 2. f6 *and* **3. Qxg7#**

#198. **1. Rg8+ Kxg8 2. Qg5+ Kf8
3. Qg7#**

#199. **1. b6+ Ka6 2. Qa8+ Kb5
3. Qa5#**

#200. **1. h4+ Kxh4 2. Rxh5+ gxh5
3. Qxh5#**

#201. **1. Qf4+ Kd5 2. c4+ Kc6
3. Qc7#**

#202. **1. Qh8+ Qg8 2. Rxf7+ Kxf7
3. Qf6#** *The swallow's tail mate.*

#203. **1. Re8** (*threatens* **2. Qg7#**)
**1...Qxe8 2. Qf6+ Rg7
3. Qxg7#**

#204. **1. Bc6+ Qxc6 (1...Kd8 2. Qd7#)
2. Rxf8+ Kxf8 3. Qxe7#**

#205. **1. Rxc8+ Bxc8 2. Bf4** *and*
3. Qb8#

#206. **1. Qh6+ Ke8 (1...Kg8 2. Qg7#)
2. Qh8+ Kd7 3. Qd8#**

#207. **1. Nc7+ Qxc7 2. Qe6+ Be7
3. Qxe7#**

#208. **1. Rh4 Rg7 2. Bf8** *and the
Queen mates on g7 or h7.*

#209. **1. Qf4+ Kg8 2. Qf7+ Kh8
3. Qg7#**

#210. **1. Qxd6+ Kg8 2. Re8+ Qf8
3. Qxf8#**

#211. **1. Bf8** (*threatens* **2. Qxa7#**)
**1...Rb7
2. Rd8+ Rb8 3. Qxa7#**

#212. **1. Bxh5** (*threatens* **2. Qg6#**)
1...Kxh5 2. Qh7+ Kg4 3. Qh3#

#213. **1. Bxh7+ Nxh7 (1...Kh8 2.Nf7#)
2. Qf7+ Kh8 3. Ng6#**

#214. **1. Bxd4+ Nxd4 2. Qf6+ Kg8
3. Nh6#**

#215. **1. Nb3 h2 2. Kb6 h1/Q
3. Nc5#**

#216. **1. Ne2 Ka1 2. Nc1 a2
3. Nb3#**

#217. **1. Rh3 gxh3 (1...g3 2. Ng4#)
2. Ng4 h2 3 Nf2#**

#218. **1. Qxh7+ Nxh7 2. Nxf7+ Nxf7
3. Ng6#**
*White's 1st and 2nd moves can be re-
versed.*

#219. **1. Nd6+ Kd8 (1...Kf8 2. Qh6#)
2. Qe8+ Rxe8 3. Nf7#**

#220. **1.Qxb8+Bxb8 (1...Kxb8 2.Rc8#)
2. Nb6+ Ka7 3. Ndc8#**

#221. **1. Rxa6+ bxa6 2. b7+ Ka7**
3. b8/Q#

#222. **1. Qa4+ Kxa4 2. Rxa7+ Kb5**
3 a4#

#223. **1. Qg7+ Rxg7 2. Nh6+ Kh8**
3. fxg7#

#224. **1. Bh6+ Kxh6 2. Qf8+ Kh5**
3. g4#

#225. **1. Ra6+ Kxa6 2. Nc5+ Ka5**
3. b4#

#226. **1. Rh3+ Nh5 2. Rxh5+ gxh5**
3. g5#

#227. **1. Nh5+ Kg8 2. f6 hxg5 3. f7#**

#228. **1. Qf8+ Rxf8 2. Rxf8+ Kd7**
3. e6#

#229. **1. Rh8+ Kxh8 2. Rh6+ Kg8**
3. Qxg7#

#230. **1. Rh8+ Kxh8 2. Qh6+ Bh7**
3. Qxg7#

#231. **1. Ra8+ Kxa8 2. Qa6+ Kb8**
3. Qxb7#

#232. **1. Qg8+ Kh6 2. Qdf8+ Qg7**
3. Qh8#

#233. **1. Qxh6+ Kg8 (1...Kxh6**
2.Bxf6#) **2. Bxf6 Rh7** (*else*
Queen mates at g7 or h8)
3. Qxh7# *A pin mate.*

#234. **1. Qxf7+ Kxf7 2. R1h7+ Ke8**
3. Bg6#

#235. **1. Qh8+ Kxh8 2. Nxf7+ Kg8**
3. Nh6#

#236. **1. Qe8+ Kxe8 2. Nf6+ Kd8**
3. Re8#

#237. **1. Qh6+ Bxh6 2. Ng5+ Kh8**
3. Rh7#

#238. **1. Qe8+ Kxe8 2. Bc6+ Kf8**
3. Re8#

#239. **1. Qe8+ Kxe8 2. Bb5+ Kd8**
3. Re8#

#240. **1. Qd8+ Kxd8 2. Bg5+ Ke8**
3. Rd8#

#241. **1. Qg8+ Kxg8 2. Be6+ Kh8**
3. Rg8#

#242. **1. Rxg7+ Kxg7 2. Rg8+ Kxg8**
3. Rg1#

#243. **1. Rf8+ Rxf8 2. Rxg6+ Rf6**
3. Bxf6#

#244. **1. Kc2 Nd2 2. Nd4 N-moves**
3. Nb3#

#245. **1. Kf6 cxd6 2. Ke7 dxc5**
3. Nf6#

#246. **1. Kd3 (A) 1...Kc5 2. Qa5#**
(B) 1...Ke5 2. Qg5#
(C) 1...c5 2. Qg5+ e5 3. Qg8#
(D) 1...e5 2. Qa5+ c5 3. Qa8#

#247. **1. Bf2 Kb4 2. Bd4 Ka3 3.Bc5#**
A little King and Bishop duel.
Bishop wins.

#248. **1. Bh1 f4 2. Bxe4 f3 3.Bxb7#**
A Bishop and Pawn duel. No contest. Bishop wins again.

#249. **1. Rc5**
(A) **1...dxc5 2. c4 dxc3 3. Nxc3#**
(B) **1...d5 2. c3 dxc3 3. Nxc3#**

#250. **1. Qg8 Rxg8 2. Bxg8 Kxc2 3. Bxh7#**

#251. **1...Rf1** (*threatens 2...Qxc1#*) **2. Rxf1 Qe1+ 3. Rxe1 Rxe1#**

#252. **1...Bf6** (*threatens 2...Qxg5#*) **2. Nf3** (*or 2. exf6 or 2. gxf6*) **2...Kg6** *and* **3...Qh7#**
Black's first move seals the 6th rank so White cannot play Qxe6 with check.

#253. **1...Qxe3+ 2. Bxe3 fxe3** *and* **3...Bf2#**

#254. **1...Qxb2+ 2. Rxb2 Bc2+ 3. Ra2 Bxc3#**

#255. **1...Qd1+ 2. Rxd1 Nc2+ 3. Nxc2 Rxd1#**

#256. **1...Bf3+ 2.Bxf3** (*or 2.Kg1 Qg2#*) **2...Be5** *and* **3...Qxh2#**

#257. **1...Qa1+ 2. Kxa1** (*2.Kc2 Qxc1#*) **2...dxc1/Q+ 3. Bb1 Qc3#**

#258. **1...f6 2. Ra1 Rg5** (*threatens 3...Rxh5#*) **3. fxg5+ fxg5#**

#259. **1...Qxg2+ 2. Kxg2 Nf4+ 3. Kg1 Nh3#**

#260. **1...Rc6+** (A) **2. Kd7 Rb6+ 3. Kd8 Rd6#**
(B) **2. Ke5 Bc2** *and* **3...f6#**

#261. **1...Bxd4+**
(A) **2. Qe3 Bxe3+ 3. Rf2** (*or 3. Kh1 Qxf1#*) **3...Ra1#**
(B) **2. cxd4 Qxf1+ 3. Kxf1 c1#**

#262. **1...Nh4+ 2. Rxh4 Rxg3+ 3. Kxg3 Re3#**

#263. **1...Qa4+** (A) **2. Kc1 Bxd3 3. Qd1 Qxa3#** (B) **2. Ke2 Bxd3+ 3. Kxd3** (or **3. Kf3 Qg4#**) **3...Qc4#**

#264. **1...Rc2** (*threatens 2...Na3#*) (A) **2. Rxc2 Rd1+ 3. Rc1 Na3#**
(B) **2. Kxc2 Rd2+ 3. Kb3 Rb2#**

#265. **1...Qxf2+ 2. Bxf2 Rxc1+ 3. Be1 Rxe1#**

#266. **1...Be4** (*threatens 2...Qg2#*) (A) **2. Qf3 Bxf3** *and* **3...Qg2#**
(B) **2. Qf1 Ne2+ 3. Qxe2 Qg2#**
From a scholastics tournament. The kid playing Black sat for over twenty minutes and worked it out.

#267. **1...Bxf3+ 2. Kxf3** (**2. Kg1 e1/Q#**) **2...e1/N+ 3. Kg4 h5#**

#268. **1...Rh1+ 2. Kxh1 Qh3+ 3. Kg1 Qxg2#**

#269. **1...Qg5** (*threatens 2...Qg2#*) (A) **2. Nxg5 Nxf2+ 3. Kg1 Nh3#**
(B) **2. Rg1 Qxg1+ 3. Nxg1 Ng3#**

#270. **1...d4+**
(A) **2. Kxd4 Qe4+ 3. Kc5 b6#**
(B) **2. cxd4 Qe4+ 3. Kd2 Qxd4#**
(C) **2. Kf4 Qe4+** *and* **3...Qg4#**

#271. **1...Nc1+ 2. Kb1 (2. Ka3 Qb3#)**
2...Qa2+ 3. Kxc1 Qa1#

#272. **1...Qa1+ 2. Ra2 Rxa4+**
3. bxa4 (or 3. Kxa4 Qxa2#)
3...Qc3# *An epaulet mate.*

#273. **1...Ba2+ 2. Kxa2 Qg8+**
3. Kb1 Qb3#

#274. **1...Re2+ 2. Nxe2 Ne4+**
3. Kd1 Nf2#

#275. **1...Qxe4** *(threatens 2...Nxg2+ and 3...Qe1#)*
2. dxe4 d3 *and*
3...Re2# *is unstoppable.*

#276. **1...Ra1+ 2. Bxa1 Qa7** *and*
3...Qa2#

#277. **1...Bd8+ 2. Bxd8 (2. g5 Bxg5#**
2...e1/N *with* **3...Ng2#** *or else*
3...Nf3#

#278. **1...Be4** *(threatens both 2...Qxd4# and 2...Rb1#)*
2. Rxe4 Qh1+
3. Qd1 Qxd1#

#279. **1...Ng5** *(releases stalemate and creates zugzwang)*
2. hxg5 Bxb6
3. g6 Be3#

#280. **1...Qc4+ 2. Kd6 (2. Kb6 Qb4#)**
2...Qc7+ 3. Kxd5 Qc6#

#281. **1...Qb5+ 2. Ka3 Rc4** *(threatens 3...Ra4#)* **3. Qd1 Qb4#**

#282. **1...Kc7** *followed by* **2...Ra8** *and* **3...Ra1#** *Not* **1...Rxf7?** *when White can drag things out by* **2. Ne7!**

#283. **1...Nd2+ (A) 2. Kb2 Qb1+**
3. Kc3 Ne4# (B) 2. Kc1 Qb1+
3. Kxd2 Bb4#
A switch back combined with a criss-cross mate.

#284. **1...Qa4** *(threatens 2...Qxa2#)*
(A) 2. a3 Qxb3+ 3. Ka1
Rxa3# (B) 2. bxa4 Rb6+ 3.
Ka1 Nc2# (C) 2. Kb2 (or 2.
Re3) 2...Qxa2+ *and* **3...Qc2#**

#285. **1...Rd2+ 2. Nxd2 Qa2+** *and*
3...Qxd2#

#286. **1...Qxb2+ 2. Nxb2 Nc3+**
3. Ka1 Nxc2#

#287. **1...Qxb2 (A) 2. Rxb2 Rc1+**
3. Rb1 b2# (B) 2. Kxb2 Rc2+
and **3...Rxa2#**

#288. **1.Rg1+ 2. Kxg1 Rg8+**
3. Kf2 Rg2#

#289. **1...Bb3** *(threatens 2...Qxa2#)*
2. cxb3 (2. axb3 Qa1#)
2...Rc1+ 3. Rxc1 Rxc1#

#290. **1...Qh3+ 2. Kxh3 Bf1+**
3. Kh4 f5#

#291. **1...Rxa3+ 2. Kxa3 Qc5+**
3. Ka2 Qa7#
Greco's mating pattern on the Rook's file.

#292. 1...Qa5+ 2. Ba4 Qxa4+
3. bxa4 Ra3#

#293. 1...Rxc2+ 2. Bxc2 Qb4+
3. Ke3 Qd4#

#294. 1...Nb3+ 2. axb3 Qa3+
3. bxa3 Ra2#

#295. 1...Rxb3+ 2. cxb3
(2. Ka2 Rb2#)
2...Qd3+ 3. Ka2 Qxb3#

#296. 1...Bb7 (*threatens* 2...h1/Q#)
(A) 2. Kh7 Rg4 *and* 3...h1/Q#
(B) 2. Rxb7 h1/Q+ 3. Rh7
Qa8#

#297. 1...Re3+ 2. Kxd4 Nc2+
3. Kc4 b5#

#298. 1...Nxc2+ 2. Kb1 Nd4+
3. Kc1 (*or* 3. Ka1 Nb3#)
3...Ne2#

#299. 1...Ba8 2. b7 Kxb7
3. Kd5 Qe5#

#300. 1...Rf1+ 2. Kxf1 Qh1+
3. Kf2 Ng4#

#301. 1. Be4+ Kg5 2. Rg7+ Kh6
3. Rh7+ Kg5 4. h4#

#302. 1. Rxa7+ Kxa7 2. Rb7+ Ka8
3. Ra7+ Kxa7 4. Qb7#

#303. 1. Qh6+ Kxh6 2. Ng4+ Kg7
3. Nh5+ Kh8 4. g7#

BEGINNING AND GENERAL CHESS BOOKS -

THE BASICS OF WINNING CHESS *by Jacob Cantrell* - A great first book of chess, in one easy reading, beginner's learn the moves, pieces, basic rules and principles of play, standard openings, and both Algebraic and English chess notation. The basic ideas of the winning concepts and strategies of middle and end game play are also shown. Includes example games of champions. 64 pages, $4.95.

BEGINNING CHESS PLAY *by Bill Robertie* - Step-by-step approach uses 113 diagrams to teach the basics of chess: opening, middle and endgame strategies, principles of development, pawn structure, checkmates, openings and defenses, how to write and read chess notation, join a chess club, play in tournaments, use a chess clock, and get rated. Two annotated games illlustrate strategic thinking for easy learning. 144 pages, $9.95.

KEENE ON CHESS *by Raymond Keene* - Complete step-by-step course shows how to play and deepen one's understanding of chess while keeping the game fun and exciting. Fascinating chapters on chess heroes and lessons one can learn from these greats, basic chess openings, strategy, tactics, the best games of chess ever played, and the history of chess round out a player's education. Readers also learn how to use chess notation and all the basic concepts of game play – castling, pawn promotion, putting an opponent into check, the five ways of drawing or stalemating games, en passant, actual checkmate; much more. 320 pages, $18.95.

OFFICIAL RULES OF CHESS Professional, Scholastic, and Internet Chess Rules *Eric Schiller and Richard Peterson* - This is the official new guide to the professional, scholastic, amateur, and internet rules of chess for the new milennium. Players learn everything they need to know about tournaments, rating systems, etiquette for in-person and online play, chess notation, and the rules that apply to every tournament form of chess, from scholastic competitions to World Championship play. Endorsed by the CEA, the official body for U.S. scholastic chess and written by International Arbiter Eric Schiller, who has officiated at U.S., World and Olympiad Championship matches, and Richard Peterson, Exec. Director of CEA. 96 pgs, $9.95.

WHIZ KIDS TEACH CHESS *Eric Schiller & the Whiz Kids* - Today's greatest young stars, some perhaps to be future world champions, present a fascinating look at the world of chess. Each tells of their successes, failures, world travels, and love of chess, show off their best moves, and admit to their most embarrassing blunders. This is more than just a fascinating look at prodigies like Vinay Bhat and Irina Krush, it's also a primer featuring diagrams, explanations, and winning ideas for young players. 144 oversized pages, $14.95.

- OPENING STRATEGY -

COMPLETE DEFENSE TO KING PAWN OPENINGS *by Eric Schiller* - Learn a complete defensive system against 1.e4. This powerful repertoire not only limits White's ability to obtain any significant opening advantage but allows Black to adopt the flexible Caro-Kann formation, the favorite weapon of many of the greatest chess players. All White's options are explained in detail, and a plan is given for Black to combat them all. Analysis is up-to-date and backed by examples drawn from games of top stars. Detailed index lets you follow the opening from the point of a specific player, or through its history. 240 pages, $16.95.

COMPLETE DEFENSE TO QUEEN PAWN OPENINGS *by Eric Schiller* - This aggressive counterattacking repertoire covers Black opening systems against virtually every chess opening except for 1.e4 (including most flank games), based on the exciting and powerful Tarrasch Defense, an opening that helped bring Championship titles to Kasparov and Spassky. Black learns to effectively use the Classical Tarrasch, Symmetrical Tarrasch, Asymmetrical Tarrasch, Marshall and Tarrasch Gambits, and Tarrasch without Nc3, to achieve an early equality or even an outright advantage in the first few moves. 288 pages, $16.95.

GAMBIT OPENING REPERTOIRE FOR BLACK *by Eric Schiller* - For players that like exciting no-holds-barred chess, this versatile gambit repertoire shows Black how to take charge with aggressive attacking defenses against any ortho- dox White opening move; 1.e4, 1.d4 and 1.c4. Learn the Scandinavian Gambit against 1.e4, the Schara Gambit and Queen's Gambit Declined variations against 1.d4, and some flank and unorthodox gambits also. Black learns the secrets of seizing the initiative from White's hands, usually by investing a pawn or two, to begin powerful attacks that can send White to early defeat. 176 pgs, $14.95.

GAMBIT OPENING REPERTOIRE FOR WHITE *by Eric Schiller* - Chessplayers who enjoy attacking from the very first move are rewarded here with a powerful repertoire of brilliant gambits. Starting off with 1.e4 or 1.d4 and then using such sharp weapons such as the Göring Gambit (Accepted and Declined), Halasz Gambit, Alapin Gambit, Ulysses Gambit, Short Attack and many more to put great pressure on opponents. You'll learn a complete attacking repertoire to use against popular defenses such as the Sicilian, French, Scandinavian, Caro- Kann, Pirc, Alekhine, and other Open Game positions. 192 pgs, $14.95.

HYPERMODERN OPENING REPERTOIRE FOR WHITE *by Eric Schiller* - In- stead of placing pawns in the center of the board as traditional openings advise, this complete opening repertoire for White shows how to stun opponents by "allowing" Black to occupy the center with its pawns, while building a crushing phalanx from the flanks, ready to smash the center apart with Black's slightest mistake. White's approach is easy to learn because White almost always devel- ops pieces in the same manner, but can be used against all defenses no matter what Black plays! Diagrams and explanations illustrate every concept with games from the greatest players showing the principles in action.The Réti and English openings, which form the basis of the Hypermodern, lead to lively games with brilliant sacrifices and subtle maneuvering. 304 pgs, $16.95.

SECRETS OF THE KING'S INDIAN *by Eduard Gufeld and Eric Schiller* - The King's Indian is the single most popular opening and offers great opportunities for spectacular attacks and clever defenses. You'll learn fundamental concepts, critical ideas, and hidden resources along with opening traps and typical tactical and strategic mistakes. All major variations are covered including the Classical, Petrosian, Saemisch, Averbakh, Four Pawns, Fianchetto, and unconventional lines. Learn how strategies and tactics that were applied in the brilliant games of the most famous players can apply to your own game. 240 pgs, $14.95.

SECRETS OF THE SICILIAN DRAGON by *GM Eduard Gufeld and Eric Schiller* - The mighty Dragon Variation of the Sicilian Defense is one of the most exciting openings in chess. Everything from opening piece formation to the endgame, including clear explanations of all the key strategic and tactical ideas, is covered in full conceptual detail. Instead of memorizing a jungle of variations, you learn the really important ideas behind the opening, and how to adapt them at the chessboard. Section on the heroes of the Dragon shows how the greatest players handle the opening. The best book on the Dragon! 208 pgs, $14.95.

WINNING CHESS OPENINGS *by Bill Robertie* - Shows concepts and best opening moves of more than 25 openings from Black's and White's perspectives: King's Gambit, Center Game, Scotch Game, Giucco Piano, Vienna Game, Bishop's Opening, Ruy Lopez, French, Caro-Kann, Sicilian, Alekhine, Pirc, Modern, Queen's Gambit, Nimzo-Indian, Queen's Indian, Dutch, King's Indian, Benoni, English, Bird's, and Reti's, and King's Indian Attack. Examples from 25 grandmasters and champions including Fischer and Kasparov. 144 pages, $9.95

- OPENING REFERENCE -

GAMBIT CHESS OPENINGS (GCO) *by Eric Schiller* - Gambits, where one side sacrifices material for an advance in development, are the most exciting and popular openings in chess! GCO presents every important gambit opening and variation ever played and currently in vogue – more than 2,000 opening strategies in all! Each gambit is covered in detail with a diagram showing the standard position representative of the gambit, the move orders taken to reach there, and an explanation in plain language of the thinking behind the moves. More than 100 complete games are included so that you can see how the ideas behind the gambit are influential not only in the beginning of the game, but later on in its development. 784 pgs, $24.95.

STANDARD CHESS OPENINGS (SCO) *by Eric Schiller* - The new definitive standard on opening chess play in the 20th century, this comprehensive guide covers every important chess opening and variation ever played and currently in vogue. In all, more than 3,000 opening strategies are presented! Differing from previous opening books which rely almost exclusively on bare notation, *SCO* features substantial discussion and analysis on each opening so that you learn and understand the concepts behind them. Includes more than 250 completely annotated games (including a game representative of each major opening) and more than 1,000 diagrams! For modern players at any level, this is the standard reference book necessary for competitive play. *A must have for serious chess players!!!* 768 pages, $24.95

UNORTHODOX CHESS OPENINGS *by Eric Schiller* - The exciting guide to all the major unorthodox openings used by chess players, contains more than 1,500 weird, contentious, controversial, unconventional, arrogant, and outright strange opening strategies. From their tricky tactical surprises to their bizarre names, these openings fly in the face of tradition. You'll meet such openings as the Orangutang, Raptor Variation, Halloween Gambit, Double Duck, Frankenstein-Dracula Variation, and even the Drunken King! These openings are a sexy and exotic way to spice up a game and a great weapon to spring on unsuspecting and often unprepared opponents. More than 750 diagrams show essential positions. 528 pages, $24.95

WORLD CHAMPION OPENINGS *by Eric Schiller* - This serious reference work covers the essential opening theory and moves of every major chess opening and variation as played by *all* the world champions. Reading as much like an encyclopedia of the must-know openings crucial to every chess player's knowledge as a powerful tool showing the insights, concepts and secrets as used by the greatest players of all time. WCO covers an astounding 100 crucial openings in full conceptual detail (with 100 games from the champions themselves)! *A must-have book for serious players.* 400 pgs, $21.95.

- MIDDLEGAME/TACTICS/WINNING CONCEPTS -

10 MOST COMMON CHESS MISTAKES and How to Fix Them *by Larry Evans* - This fascinating collection of 218 errors, oversights, and outright blunders, not only shows the price great players pay for violating basic principles but how to avoid these mistakes in your own game. You'll be challenged to choose between two moves, the right one or the one actually played. From neglecting development, king safety, misjudging threats and premature attacks, to impulsiveness, snatching pawns, and basic inattention, you receive a complete course in where you can go wrong and how to fix it. 256 pgs, $14.95.

100 AWESOME CHESS MOVES *By Eric Schiller* - This collection of brilliant ideas from real tournaments are not just regular combinations or tactical swindles, but moves of stunning originality. Schiller has selected 100 awesome moves, and through game positions, examples, and clearly explained concepts, shows players how to improve their grasp of deep positional understandings and swashbuckling tactics. Readers learn how to reinforce their gut instincts to not just reach for the best move, but the *inspired* move. 288 pages, $18.95.

303 TRICKY CHESS TACTICS *Fred Wilson and Bruce Alberston* - Both a fascinating challenge and great training tool, this is a fun and entertaining collection of two and three move tactical surprises for the advanced beginner, intermediate, and expert player. Tactics are arranged by difficulty so that a player may measure progress as he advances from simple to the complex positions. The examples, drawn from actual games, illustrate a wide range of chess tactics from old classics right up to the 1990's. 192 pages, $12.95.

ENCYCLOPEDIA OF CHESS WISDOM, The Essential Concepts and Strategies of Smart Chess Play *by Eric Schiller* - The most important concepts, strategies, tactics, wisdom, and thinking that every chessplayer must know, plus the gold nuggets of knowledge behind every attack and defense is collected together in one volume. Step-by-step, from opening, middle and endgame strategy, to psychological warfare and tournament tactics, Schiller shows the thinking behind each essential concept, and through examples, diagrams, and discussions, shows its impact on the game. 432 pages, $19.95.

TEST YOUR CHESS I. Q. - 100 great chess challenges test your true chess level! *by Larry Evans* - Test your skills against 100 fascinating positions from actual games and choose the best move from among three choices. After completing the challenges, you can calculate your rating - be it beginner or grandmaster! In the solutions section, chess great Larry Evans explains why the lesser alternatives available to you are inferior and how to analyze the position for maximum understanding. You'll learn from all the elements that make up victory or defeat to find your true chess level. 144 pgs, $12.95.

DEVELOPMENT OF A CHESS MASTER *by Eric Schiller* - The thinking player's guide that shows you how to take your game to the next level by cutting down on tactical and strategic mistakes. Using examples from his own games, Schiller illustrates the types of errors typically found at each stage of chess development, from early scholastic games to professional encounters with Grandmasters. In each case, Schiller shows how such errors can be overcome while at the same time showing how professional players can fall prey to the same problems as amateurs. Learn from the author's mistakes and you won't suffer the terrible fate that awaits most blunders! 192 pages, $14.95.

WINNING CHESS TACTICS *by Bill Robertie* - 14 chapters of winning ideas show the complete thinking behind every tactical concept: pins, single and double forks, double attacks, skewers, discovered and double checks, multiple threats, plus other crushing tactics to gain an edge over opponents. Learn the power tools of tactical play to become a better player. Includes guide to chess notation. 128 pgs, $9.95.

WORLD CHAMPION COMBINATIONS *by Raymond Keene and Eric Schiller* - Learn the insights, concepts, and moves of the greatest combinations ever by the best players of all time. From Morphy to Alekhine, to Fischer to Kasparov, the incredible combinations and brilliant sacrifices of the 13 World Champions are collected here in the most insightful combinations book yet. Packed with fascinating strategems, 50 annotated games, and great practical advice for your own games, this is a great companion guide to the other titles in the *World Champion* series. 264 pages, $16.95.

WORLD CHAMPION TACTICS *by Leonid Shamkovich and Eric Schiller* - The authors show how the greatest players who ever lived used their entire arsenal of tactical weapons to bring opponents to their knees. Packed with fascinating strategems, 50 fully annotated games, and more than 200 diagrams, players learn not only the thinking and game plan behind the moves of the champions, but the insights that will allow them to use these brilliancies in their own games. Each tactical concept is fully explained with examples and game situations from the champions themselves. 304 pages, $18.95.

- MATES & ENDGAMES -
303 TRICKY CHECKMATES *by Fred Wilson and Bruce Alberston* - Both a fascinating challenge and great training tool, this collection of two, three and bonus four move checkmates is great for advanced beginning, intermediate and expert players. Mates are in order of difficulty, from simple to complex positions. Learn the standard patterns and strategems for cornering the king: corridor and support mates, attraction and deflection sacrifices, pins and annihilation, the quiet move, and the dreaded *zugzwang*. Examples from actual games illustrate a wide range of tactics from classics right up to the 1990's. 192 pages, $12.95.

BASIC ENDGAME STRATEGY: Kings, Pawns and Minor Pieces *by Bill Robertie* - Learn the mating principles and combinations needed to finish off opponents. From the four basic checkmates using the King with the queen, rook, two bishops, and bishop/knight combinations, to the King/pawn, King/Knight and King/Bishop endgames, you'll learn how to translate small edges into decisive checkmates. Shows the 50-move rule, and the combinations of pieces that can't force a mate against a lone King. 144 pgs, $12.95.

BASIC ENDGAME STRATEGY: Rooks and Queens *by Bill Robertie* - The companion guide to *Basic Endgame: Kings, Pawns and Minor Pieces*, you'll learn the basic mating principles and combinations of the Queen and Rook with King, how to turn middlegame advantages into victories by creating passed pawns, using the King as a weapon, clearing the way for rook mates, and other strategems. 144 pgs, $12.95.

639 ESSENTIAL ENDGAME POSITIONS *by Eric Schiller* - From basic checkmates to sophisticated double-rook endgames, every important endgame concept is explained. Topics include every key combination of king and pawn endgames, bishops, knights, rooks, and queens, plus tricky endgames with no pawns. The thinking behind every position is explained in words (unlike diagram-only books) so that players learn which positions are winning, which are drawn, and which cannot be saved. Frequent diagrams show starting and target positions so readers can visualize end goals and steer the middlegame to a successful conclusion. 400 pages, $18.95.

MASTER CHECKMATE STRATEGY *by Bill Robertie* - Learn the basic combinations, plus advanced, surprising and unconventional mates, the most effective pieces needed to win, and how to mate opponents with just a pawn advantage. also, how to work two rooks into an unstoppable attack; how to wield a queen advantage with deadly intent; how to coordinate pieces of differing strengths into indefensible positions of their opponents; when it's best to have a knight, and when a bishop to win. 144 pages, $9.95

For a complete list of Cardoza chess titles, go to our website
www.cardozapub.com

Also, visit Chess City, our free online chessmagazine!
www.chesscity.com

Use the order form below or call toll-free
(800)577-WINS
Get your chess books now!

BECOME A BETTER CHESS PLAYER!

YES! I want to be a winner! Rush me the following items: (Write in choices below):

Quantity	Your Book Order	Price	

MAKE CHECKS TO:
Cardoza Publishing
P. O. Box 1500, Cooper Station
NY, NY 10276

CHARGE BY PHONE:
Toll-Free: 1-800-577-WINS
Local Phone: 718-743-5229
Fax Orders: 718-743-8284
E-Mail Orders: CardozaPub@aol.com

Subtotal		
Postage/Handling: First Item	$5	00
Additional Postage		
Total Amount Due		

SHIPPING CHARGES: For US orders, include $5.00 postage/handling 1st book ordered; for each additional book, add $1.00. For Canada/Mexico, double above amounts, quadruple (4X) for all other countries. Orders outside U.S., money order payable in U.S. dollars on U.S. bank only.

NAME _____

ADDRESS _____

CITY _____ STATE _____ ZIP _____

30 day money back guarantee!   303 Mates 2002

CARDOZA PUBLISHING ONLINE
www.cardozapub.com

We welcome your suggestions and comments, and are glad to have you as a customer. Our philosophy is to bring you the best quality chess books from the top authors and authorities in the chess world, featuring *words* (as opposed to hieroglyphics), *clear expanations* (as opposed to gibberish), *nice presentations* (as opposed to books simply slapped together), and authoritative information. And all this at reasonable prices.

We hope you like the results.

Don't forget to try out the companion book by Wilson and Alberston:
303 Tricky Tactics

To find out about our newest chess and backgammon books or to order chess sets, clocks or other accessories:
Go online: www.cardozapub.com
Use email: cardozapub@aol.com
Call toll free: (800)577-9467

FREE - CHESS CITY MAGAZINE
www.chesscity.com

Go online now to visit our free online chess magazine with articles, columns, gossip, and more. The web's most interesting and informative chess magazine is free to you from Cardoza Publishing!